Awfully Good
PUZZLES

STUDIO
PRESS

Designed by Rob Ward and Collaborate
Illustrations by Collaborate and Shutterstock.com

© 2017 Studio Press
An imprint of Kings Road Publishing
Part of Bonnier Publishing
The Plaza, 535 King's Road, London, SW10 0SZ
www.bonnierpublishing.co.uk

Printed in the United Kingdom   10 9 8 7 6 5 4 3 2 1

BORED CHAP

CHALLENGE BOOK

RAF Silhouettes

Earn your pilot wings by naming these Royal Air Force plane silhouettes.

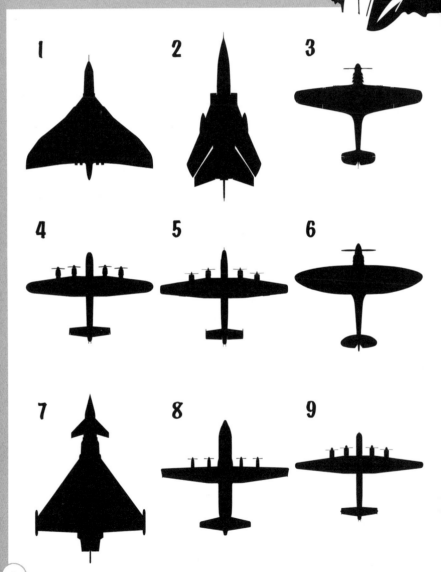

CAR PARTS WORD SEARCH

U	W	E	E	H	Q	K	T	O	S	E	E	F	I	E
N	B	N	O	I	T	I	N	G	I	B	R	P	S	L
Q	E	S	J	I	R	D	F	T	Y	E	L	C	W	K
M	E	U	R	A	D	I	A	T	O	R	E	A	S	I
N	A	K	N	E	R	C	O	Y	V	S	T	R	Q	S
A	K	C	I	T	S	P	I	D	S	P	F	B	Q	L
Y	M	Q	Z	U	W	J	U	T	P	E	L	U	R	X
R	P	U	S	H	R	O	D	S	A	I	A	R	Z	O
E	G	N	K	E	V	S	D	U	R	T	S	E	T	J
T	I	R	N	N	R	G	Q	A	K	W	F	T	M	W
T	N	W	A	T	A	N	O	H	P	H	X	T	O	D
A	Z	E	T	S	T	R	G	X	L	M	N	O	E	N
B	R	X	P	D	S	C	C	E	U	R	H	R	B	V
D	Z	V	A	L	V	E	J	Z	G	I	E	K	D	P
J	N	O	T	F	I	P	D	P	S	B	G	L	L	X

SPARK PLUGS
CARBURETTOR
VALVE
PISTON
CRANK
HOSE

EXHAUST
PUSH ROD
DIPSTICK
RADIATOR
BATTERY
IGNITION

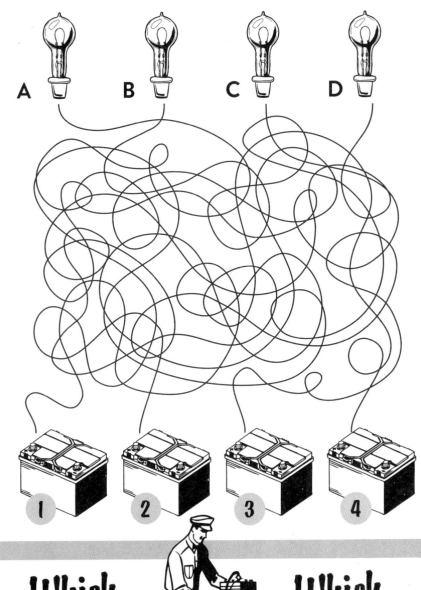

A B C D

1 2 3 4

Which Which
LIGHT TO BATTERY?

DOT TO DOT

Join up the dots to complete this truly rockin' dot to dot!

Match THESE CAPITALS

Countries	Capitals
LITHUANIA	BRAZZAVILLE
REP. OF CONGO	TALLINN
TURKMENISTAN	ASHGABAT
ESTONIA	ASUNCIÓN
GABON	DUSHANBE
TAJIKISTAN	LIBREVILLE
PARAGUAY	QUITO
ECUADOR	VILNIUS

Which capital city is this?

S _ F _ A

TRY THESE *sensational* SUDOKU

EASY

2			8		4			6
		6				5		
	7	4				9	2	
3				4				7
			3		5			
4				6				9
	1	9				7	4	
		8				2		
5			6		8			1

EASY

	3		9				2	
8					2			7
		1	4			6		
	9			4		5		2
			6		3			
7		6		1			8	
	9				4	1		
2			8					3
	7				9		5	

MEDIUM

		4	7	2				9
	2	6		8	4	1		
8								
	9	7		1				
			6		8			
			3			7	6	
								2
	5	2	6			4	1	
7				5	1	3		

"These two are dastardly hard!"

HARD

					2	7	5	
	1	8		9				
4	9							
	3							8
			7			2		
				3				9
7								
5							8	

HARD

	4	6	5	1	2			3
	2			6			1	
1				9	4			
5				7	2			
	7		8				9	
	9	2						8
	7	3						6
	9			2			5	
4				8	3			

SPOT THE Difference

Word Scramble
VOLCANOES

Can you unjumble these famous hot heads?

ANETTUNMO ....

FUNMIJUOT ....

KAATAKOR ....

TSMSHEUNNOTLE ....

IOTNVUUVSSMUE ....

USOMPMNUTLYO ....

TUPNTOAUOBNMI ....

AABROUMNMTTO ....

BIRDS *of the* WORLD WORD SEARCH

P	O	K	R	B	Y	K	U	V	L	H	E	O	O	C
E	P	O	S	T	R	I	C	H	Q	C	W	B	V	R
O	G	N	I	M	A	L	F	K	T	H	Z	I	D	Q
I	Y	T	Y	D	L	S	L	X	D	U	B	D	S	H
O	G	O	K	D	N	T	N	N	M	I	O	R	L	G
C	T	U	D	K	Z	P	I	E	I	E	Q	I	Q	O
Q	F	C	N	I	L	E	N	J	F	U	A	B	X	D
L	G	A	I	W	D	L	E	T	D	O	G	G	I	J
C	D	N	F	I	Y	I	I	B	P	L	L	N	L	A
J	Q	F	F	I	F	C	B	B	O	N	B	I	E	E
C	C	G	U	L	S	A	R	O	N	S	R	M	I	P
G	N	B	P	P	Z	N	R	O	R	A	M	W	Z
X	S	Z	R	P	C	A	B	T	N	K	O	U	T	G
K	V	E	U	T	M	B	V	U	O	X	I	H	X	N
U	V	U	L	T	U	R	E	D	K	S	Z	S	U	N

KIWI
OSTRICH
TOUCAN
PELICAN
FLAMINGO
HORNBILL

PENGUIN
HUMMINGBIRD
PUFFIN
VULTURE
EAGLE
EMU

POISONOUS ANIMALS of the WORLD

CLUES ON OPPOSITE PAGE!

CROSSWORD

Across:

3. Which well-camouflaged fish often stings people as a result of being stepped on? (5,4)

5. Which venomous mammal comes from the world's 'island continent'? (8)

7. Which marine mollusc uses a venomous harpoon to capture prey? (4,5)

10. Which rainforest dweller's bright colouring is indicative of its toxicity levels? (6,4,4)

11. Which marine stinger is named after its cube-like shape? (3,9)

13. Which African reptile gets its name from its skin colour? (5,5)

Down:

1. Which reptile's name means 'tree snake' in Afrikaans? (9)

2. Which reptile is the only venomous lizard native to the United States? (4,7)

4. Which creepy-crawly is identifiable by a reddish hourglass-shaped marking on its abdomen? (5,5)

6. Which fish contains tetrodotoxin, a substance 1,200 times more poisonous than cyanide? (10)

8. Which Indonesian lizard shares the name of the island it is from? (6,6)

9. Which regal snake is endemic to Asia? (4,5)

12. Which fish is named after the king of the jungle? (4,4)

A. BOWLER   D. TOP HAT   G. TRILBY
B. FLAT CAP   E. BOBBLE HAT   H. PANAMA
C. FEDORA   F. PORK PIE HAT I. BERET

1

2

3

4

5

6

7

8

9

MATCH That Hat

Road Chat

LEICESTER to CANTERBURY

Roads

Which nine roads will get you from the centre of Leicester to the centre of Canterbury the fastest?

A47	A14	A26
M25	A428	A120
A2	A423	M26
M2	A509	A2050
A43	M11	M1
A4010	M3	A5460
A20	M20	A282

___ _____

__ ___ ____ __

__ __ _____

QUESTIONS

1 How can a bucket be empty but still have something in it?

....

2 Two doctors say that Harry is their brother. Harry says he has no brothers. Who is lying?

....

3 What occurs twice in an instant, once in a moment and yet never in a day?

....

4 Paul lies every Monday, Tuesday and Wednesday. James lies on Thursdays, Fridays and Saturdays. Paul says, 'Yesterday I was lying'. James says, 'So was I.' Which day did they say that on?

....

5 A boat has a ladder with 10 rungs. The rungs are 20cm apart. Three rungs are submerged. Overnight the water level rises by 1 metre. How many rungs are submerged in the morning?

....

Rack your brains to answer these truly complicated and pickling puzzlers!

6 Susan's dad has five daughters: May, April, June and July. What's the fifth daughter's name?

....

7 A lorry driver passes five policemen while going down a one-way street the wrong way. Why isn't he stopped?

....

8 What travels the world but never leaves its corner?

....

9 What is 1/2 monkey, 1/3 ant and 2/3 cow?

....

10 Charles is 34 years old. How many birthdays has he had?

....

11 A peacock lays an egg on a farmhouse roof. Which way does it fall?

....

List all the James Bond films.

Make sure you put them in order, not shaken up, or stirred.

1 ....
2 ....
3 ....
4 ....
5 ....
6 ....
7 ....
8 ....
9 ....
10 ....
11 ....
12 **Moonraker** ....
13 ....
14 ....
15 ....
16 **A View to a Kill** .....
17 ....

18 ....
19 ....
20 ....
21 ....
22 ....
23 ....
24 ....
25 ....
26 ....

Smart 💡 SEQUENCE

DOT TO DOT

SPACE TRAVEL

1 Buzz Aldrin's mother's maiden name was Marion Moon.

○ True ○ False

2 The astronauts forming the Apollo 13 crew were placed in quarantine once they returned to Earth.

○ True ○ False

3 The hottest planet is not the closest planet to the Sun.

○ True ○ False

4 The footprints on the Moon will likely be around for more than 100 million years.

○ True ○ False

5 Earth is the only planet with its own weather.

○ True ○ False

True OR False

6 Astronauts become taller in space.

○ True ○ False

7 Buzz Aldrin did not actually walk on the Moon.

○ True ○ False

8 The American flag that Neil Armstrong and Buzz Aldrin placed on the Moon still sits there today.

○ True ○ False

9 Astronauts are time travellers.

○ True ○ False

10 The word 'astronaut' translates as 'star sailor' in Greek.

○ True ○ False

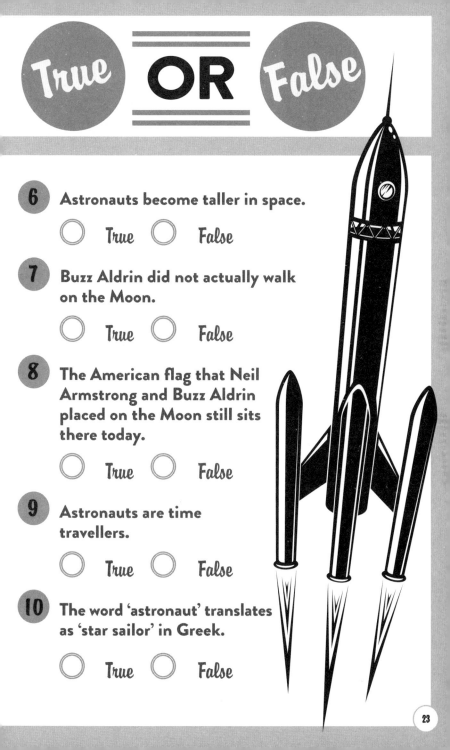

PLACES OF THE World
WORD SCRAMBLE

RAEGRARTBIFERERE ....

HHCMCUUAPIC ....

IEGTENERS ....

NNDOCRGYNAA ....

ASFOLRILCATVI ....

RMAZNEOARIV ....

OYLNEWLSTEO ....

IAZOMRFAGPSIYD ....

JMLAAHTA ....

Can you make sense of this balderdash to reveal nine famous tourist destinations?

EASY

3		2			8	6		
5		4		6				2
	6				1			9
4	2		9					
	7						3	
					2		4	1
2			3				1	
1				5		4		3
		3	6			7		8

EASY

		5	7					
	9			2				4
3	2	1	4	5	8			
6	1	3						2
2						3	6	8
		1	4	7	2	9	6	
4				6			5	
					9	4		

MEDIUM

	2		5		9	6		
		2		9				
9		5			6	1		
		8			2			9
2			5		1			3
1			3			8		
		9	7			2		1
			9		4			
	5	6		2		3		

HARD

			5		1		9	
5		2		8		7		3
		6		3			5	
7		4				6		
	2						8	
	8				5		1	
	6			1		9		
9		8		4		1		6
	4		2		6			

HARD

	9			8				
			2				9	7
	7		9	4		6		
3				6			2	
7	8	6				5	4	9
	4			8				3
		8		5	6		1	
1	6			3				
			1			8		

Spot the DIFFERENCE

CAN YOU SEEK OUT THE VANISHING ACTS?

Make like a Time Lord and see if you can list all 13 Doctor Who stars in chronological order.

1 ....

2 ....

3 ....

4 ....

5 ....

6 ....

7 ....

8 ....

9 ....

10 ....

11 ....

12 ....

13 ....

Smart 💡 SEQUENCE

Roads

Which eight roads will get you from the centre of Swindon to the centre of Brighton the fastest?

A419	A21	A205
M4	M20	A339
A346	A406	A26
A36	M25	A3102
A23	A1	A39
A417	A34	A259
A4259	A27	A217

---- -- --- ----

--- --- ---

Star
CONSTELLATIONS

CLUES ON OPPOSITE PAGE!

CROSSWORD

Across:

4. A V-shaped pattern of stars form the head of this constellation. (6)

6. Which constellation in the northern sky is named after a winged animal? (7)

8. The Plough, also known as the Big Dipper, forms part of this constellation. (4,5)

10. Which is the fifth largest constellation in the sky that goes by the Roman name for the demigod who completed 12 labours? (8)

11. Which constellation was named after the mythical princess married to the Greek hero Perseus? (9)

Down:

1. Which constellation is home to the spiral galaxy M74, some 30 million light years from Earth? (6)

2. Which constellation tells the story of Orpheus? (4)

3. Which constellation is named after the man who decapitated Medusa? (7)

5. Which handsome cup-bearer to the gods was granted a place in the sky? (8)

7. Which constellation is named after the vain and boastful queen in Greek mythology? (10)

9. Which constellation contains Altair, its most prominent star? (6)

12. Which constellation that lies on the celestial equator is also known as the hunter? (5)

1 Charles Darwin's pet tortoise Harriet died in 2006, a whole 124 years after her owner.

○ True   ○ False

2 On the 26th of May, 1868, people travelled to the last public execution held in London via the city's underground tube.

○ True   ○ False

3 In France, the guillotine as a form of capital punishment was abolished in 1972, only five years before the first *Star Wars* film was released.

○ True   ○ False

4 The Nintendo 64 was first sold before the first text message was sent.

○ True   ○ False

5 Picasso died in 1973, the same year that Bic invented their disposable lighter.

○ True   ○ False

HISTORIC DATES

6 The end of Prohibition in the United States is temporally nearer to the Apollo 11 Moon landing than the present day.

○ True ○ False

7 The first iPod was introduced the same year Facebook was launched, in 2004.

○ True ○ False

8 FIFA was founded the same year Salvador Dali was born.

○ True ○ False

9 Pluto was no longer considered a planet when Brazil last won the World Cup.

○ True ○ False

10 It took 20 years after the invention of the eraser for stationers to create the rubber-tipped pencil.

○ True ○ False

TRUE or FALSE

CARPENTRY JOINTS

Can you name these nifty carpentry joints?

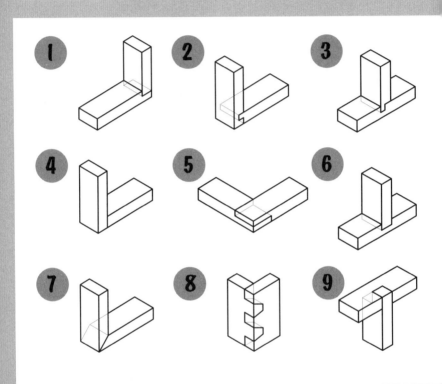

A. RABBET JOINT
B. BUTT JOINT
C. MITRE JOINT
D. TONGUE AND DADO JOINT
E. DADO RABBET JOINT
F. LAP JOINT
G. DOVETAIL JOINT
H. HALF CROSS LAP JOINT
I. THROUGH DADO JOINT

BEERS of the World

WORD SEARCH

N	M	Z	Q	B	V	O	K	C	Q	G	D	F	W	E
V	S	D	H	B	R	A	H	M	A	N	V	P	X	N
X	O	C	V	S	K	O	L	U	G	I	N	T	E	C
K	N	Z	Z	D	H	I	E	O	X	J	E	J	O	O
C	O	R	O	N	A	H	P	C	Z	N	D	T	A	O
Q	T	U	D	H	D	O	E	E	B	A	R	W	I	R
R	S	I	H	Y	B	I	O	E	E	Y	A	K	E	S
E	I	U	H	E	I	N	E	K	E	N	A	Z	D	L
G	N	B	U	D	W	E	I	S	E	R	G	E	B	I
I	G	E	C	F	Y	M	Y	H	Q	N	E	Q	G	G
T	T	R	Y	A	D	P	M	E	D	B	O	M	D	H
G	A	V	S	W	O	R	K	U	C	G	H	H	W	T
Q	O	A	G	U	I	N	N	E	S	S	G	X	E	H
R	H	W	I	S	R	T	J	I	U	V	I	N	X	K
I	G	F	E	Y	A	T	G	Z	A	M	K	K	B	L

GUINNESS   YANJING
TIGER   CORONA
HOEGAARDEN   ASAHI
COORS LIGHT   SKOL
BRAHMA   BUDWEISER
HEINEKEN   TSINGTAO

ASHES Trivia

1 If an umpire raises one leg and taps his knee with one hand, what is he signalling?

....

2 Which England bowler scored a hat-trick at Sydney during the 1998–99 tour?

○ Dean Headley   ○ Alex Tudor
○ Darren Gough   ○ Ian Botham

3 Which Australian captain twice won the Ashes on his birthday?

○ Bill Brown   ○ Ian Johnson
○ Bill Woodfull   ○ Arthur Morris

4 Who replaced his brother in an Australian Ashes team and went on to score a debut century?

○ Chris Lynn   ○ Bill Brown
○ Scott Boland   ○ Mark Waugh

5 How many matches did the 1948 Australians lose on their tour of England?

....

6 Who took 10 wickets in his final Test in January 2003?

○ Matthew Hoggard   ○ Craig White
○ Richard Dawson   ○ Andy Caddick

7 How many wickets did Tony Lock take in the Ashes Test at Old Trafford in 1956?

....

8 On average, how often is the Ashes?

....

9 In what year were the first Ashes?

....

10 Who has scored the most runs for England in an Ashes series?

....
....

11 What is Freddie Flintoff's real name?

....

EASY

			2	9	7		6	
		6						8
	3	2	6			4		1
7		5			1			
8								7
			8			3		5
4		7			3	8	5	
3					6			
	9		4	5	8			

EASY

					5	1	9	3
			7					
	4	5		1	8	2		
			5			7	6	
2	5						3	4
	6	4			9			
		8	2	6		9	1	
					1			
5	7	1	4					

MEDIUM

1	6	7	2					
3					1			9
			6			7	1	
	5			6	7			4
		3		8		9		
7			4	1			6	
	1	6			9			
4				8				6
					6	3	4	5

MEDIUM

		6		2		1	9	8
8			6	9				
	7		5				4	
	5					4	8	
2				7				6
	9	4					1	
	6				1		3	
			6	5				1
1	3	9			4		8	

HARD

5	1		2	7				
4			6		5		8	
	6	9						
				1			5	
2	8		3		4		7	9
	3			5				
						5	4	
	4		5		7			2
			2	6			1	3

HARD

	6							
9			3	6	8	4		
7				1		9		
1				9	5			8
	3	6				7	9	
8		9	7					2
		4		9				5
	1	2	5	6				9
							1	

· S · U · D · O · K · U ·

--- -- -- ---

--- --- -- ---

Roads

Which eight roads will get you from the centre of Land's End to the centre of John O'Groats the fastest?

A1	M55	A99
A82	A74	A30
M80	A93	A6006
A835	M7	M6
A92	A95	A50
A6108	M9	M73
M5	M54	A47

Road Chat 🔑 LAND'S END to JOHN O'GROATS

Name That COUNTRY

Is your knowledge world class? Identify these country silhouettes.

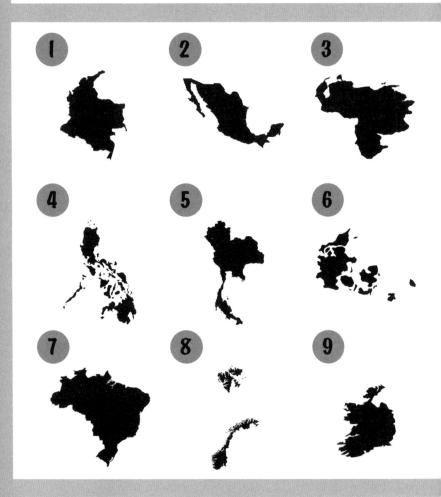

1
2
3
4
5
6
7
8
9

A. THAILAND
B. PHILIPPINES
C. IRELAND

D. COLOMBIA
E. DENMARK
F. BRAZIL

G. VENEZUELA
H. MEXICO
I. NORWAY

World's FASTEST RUNNERS

USNAIBLOT   ....

EJSSENWOSE   ....

LSAGIJUTNTIN   ....

SMIEMTTOMIH   ....

ENIREAECGREUM   ....

NENLBIAADYOOV   ....

AERCLWLIS   ....

YYTSGNOA   ....

Unscramble these names to reveal some of the speediest sprinters around!

Flex your box-office credentials by listing the last 17 Oscar® winners for Best Actor.

1 **Casey Affleck**
2 **Leonardo DiCaprio**
3 ....
4 ....
5 ....
6 ....
7 ....
8 ....
9 ....
10 ....
11 ....
12 ....
13 ....
14 ....
15 ....
16 **Denzel Washington**
17 ....

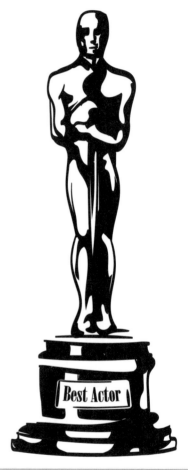

Best Actor

Smart SEQUENCE

SUPERB SUDOKU PUZZLES

EASY

		2		9	3			
1	4			3			6	
		9		8				
	5	3	4		6	8		
8				7				5
		6	5		8	7	1	
				6		4		
	7			9			2	6
		4	8		2			

EASY

			4			9		
	1		8		9		2	
5	2	9			6	4		
2	5	4						6
			7					
7						9	3	4
	7	4				5	6	3
	4		6		5		8	
	6			1				

MEDIUM

	8		5					7
	3		9		7	6	4	
				6	1	3		
		4			9			2
1				6				4
3			2			5		
	9	3	7					
	1	5	4		2		8	
7					3		9	

MEDIUM

7			9			8		2
	8		5	4		3		
	9			2		5		6
9								3
			4	3	9			
1								4
5		9		8			6	
		1		9	4		3	
3		6			2			9

HARD

				2	1	9	3	6
	9		3				1	
			6	8	9			7
7		4				5		
				5				
	5					7		3
3			5	9	4			
	2				8		6	
4	7	8	2	3				

HARD

9		3			8			
7			9		2		8	
2			4			5		
6		9	2					
4	8						1	6
				4	8			5
		4			7			8
	7		3		6			4
			8			7		3

EXPLORERS WORD SEARCH

I	T	U	I	T	T	O	C	S	T	R	E	B	O	R
F	O	I	V	K	O	L	O	P	O	C	R	A	M	C
T	A	Y	T	B	S	A	C	A	G	A	W	E	A	Y
K	P	K	V	E	A	B	C	K	P	Y	I	Y	T	U
B	E	N	E	D	I	C	T	A	L	L	E	N	A	G
Z	Z	J	A	M	E	S	C	O	O	K	V	L	F	I
H	R	Y	C	W	C	G	U	R	R	Z	F	H	X	D
E	L	M	P	A	F	Q	G	B	M	O	W	P	V	I
N	O	X	B	L	T	S	A	B	Y	N	K	F	V	N
G	P	Z	D	Y	U	R	I	G	A	G	A	R	I	N
H	W	E	T	J	O	H	N	S	M	I	T	H	V	A
E	C	L	E	K	A	R	D	S	I	C	N	A	R	F
S	N	E	I	L	A	R	M	S	T	R	O	N	G	J
D	X	A	T	U	T	T	A	B	N	B	I	S	Y	U
A	B	E	L	T	A	S	M	A	N	Q	A	B	T	E

MARCO POLO	**ROBERT SCOTT**
JAMES COOK	**FRANCIS DRAKE**
NEIL ARMSTRONG	**BENEDICT ALLEN**
JOHN SMITH	**ABEL TASMAN**
SACAGAWEA	**YURI GAGARIN**
ZHENG HE	**IBN BATTUTA**

DOT TO DOT

Have a mini adventure and complete this dot to dot!

HISTORY of DANCE

CLUES ON OPPOSITE PAGE!

CROSSWORD

Across:

3. Which dance developed in the 1910s was originally danced to ragtime? (7)

5. Which highly technical performance dance was formed during the Italian Renaissance? (6)

7. The name of this dance is also an expression meaning deceptive or foolish talk. (4)

8. Which dance style is also known as 'bashment'? (9)

10. Which 1920s dance was named after a harbour city in South Carolina? (10)

12. Which dance was shaped by dances from the Candombe ceremonies of former slave peoples? (5)

Down:

1. Which dance is primarily performed to the music of the same genre? (3,3)

2. Which dance is also called b-boying or b-girling? (10)

4. Which dance is named after a bird native to its country of origin? (8)

6. Which dance is synonymous with the names Johann Strauss, Chopin and Brahms? (5)

9. Which social dance originating in the Caribbean translates from Spanish as sauce? (5)

11. The Lindy Hop, Balboa and Collegiate Shag are styles of which dance? (5)

STRANGE
TRADITIONS

1 In the Spanish town of Buñol, masses of people flock to the streets to take part in the town's annual tomato fight.

○ True   ○ False

2 Every year in Gloucestershire, wilful participants chase a wheel of cheese down a steep hill in the hopes of reaching the bottom first to win the cheese.

○ True   ○ False

3 Devon is home to the International Festival of Wormcharming.

○ True   ○ False

4 Bog snorkelling is an annual event held in a small town in Wales.

○ True   ○ False

5 A traditional drinking game in Russia is to stand and drink rounds of vodka until someone falls or passes out.

○ True   ○ False

True or False

6 In Illinois, at the end of the harvest, tens of thousands of people travel to Peoria to participate in a yearly pumpkin-smashing event.

○ True   ○ False

7 In Denmark, broken plates and bowls are saved, and then thrown at the houses of friends and family on New Year's Eve.

○ True   ○ False

8 In Scotland, it is customary for the bride to cut off a lock of her hair and hand it to the groom as a gesture of unity.

○ True   ○ False

9 Japan hosts a penis festival every year.

○ True   ○ False

10 If you are still unmarried when you turn 25 in Denmark, it is tradition for your loved ones to throw cinnamon at you.

○ True   ○ False

Road Chat — BODMIN to STROUD

Roads

Which four roads will get you from Bodmin to the centre of Stroud the fastest?

M27	A436	A48
A303	A49	A42
M3	M5	A419
M25	A5	M1
A40	A46	A35
A30	A34	A432
A449	M6	M74

_ _ _   _ _

_ _ _ _   _ _ _

Word Scramble
GREEK PHILOSOPHERS

Can you unjumble the names of these clever thinkers?

LPAOT ....

AIRTOSTEL ....

PYTORAHAGS ....

RAHCEIMEDS ....

SORACSTE ....

TATICUS ....

EPMCEEDOLS ....

ALTHSE ....

Spot the DIFFERENCE

TAKE A GOOD LOOK FOR **10 CHANGES ON THE ROAD.**

NATURE'S
FASTEST and SLOWEST

1 What fish can only travel 1.5 metres per hour, making it the slowest-moving fish?

....

2 What is slower: a starfish or a slug?

....

3 What is the slowest animal in the world?

....

4 The fastest fish can travel up to how many miles per hour?

○ 68mph   ○ 72mph
○ 87mph   ○ 53mph

5 What is the fastest-moving fish?

○ Tuna fish   ○ Sailfish
○ Shark   ○ Barracuda

6 What is the maximum speed a cheetah can reach?

....

7 Which is faster at maximum speed: a zebra or a greyhound?

....

8 Which sea creature is also known as the 'sea cow' because it's so slow?

....

9 Which type of bird is the fastest in the world?

....

10 Which animal is the second fastest in the cat family and can reach up to 50 miles per hour?

....

11 Which animal can travel faster: the grizzly bear or the giraffe?

....

12 Which animal can only travel at a maximum speed of 5 miles per hour? These creatures are not in a rush as they can reach over 180 years of age!

....

Be a good sport, name the last 10 men to win gold in the Olympic 100m sprint.

1   **Usain Bolt** ....

2   ....

3   ....

4   ....

5   ....

6   ....

7   ....

8   ....

9   **Carl Lewis** ....

10   ....

Smart SEQUENCE

Who SAID ??? WHAT

Quotes

1. 'Not everything that can be counted counts, and not everything that counts can be counted.'

2. 'You may not be interested in war, but war is interested in you.'

3. 'Do or do not. There is no "try".'

4. 'My advice to you is get married: if you find a good wife you'll be happy; if not, you'll become a philosopher.'

5. 'You must be the change you wish to see in the world.'

6. 'Wine is constant proof that God loves us and loves to see us happy.'

7. 'I mean, part of the beauty of me is that I'm very rich.'

8. 'I have never let my schooling interfere with my education.'

9. 'I'd be a vegetarian if bacon grew on trees.'

10. 'History will be kind to me for I intend to write it.'

People

A Homer Simpson

B Winston Churchill

C Leon Trotsky

D Benjamin Franklin

E Mark Twain

F Gandhi

G Socrates

H Albert Einstein

I Yoda

J Donald Trump

Cracking CARS

WORD SEARCH

D	N	Q	I	U	X	Z	I	T	L	N	L	G	I	O
M	I	J	S	P	V	Q	G	Y	Z	O	E	Q	N	D
E	T	F	I	S	B	F	D	L	L	P	I	D	I	C
Y	C	O	I	T	T	A	G	U	B	H	T	E	H	R
N	E	Y	E	C	A	Y	H	R	Z	Y	E	J	G	C
T	R	P	O	G	N	R	H	A	O	R	Y	A	R	I
F	K	B	G	R	U	Y	E	Y	F	P	A	G	O	J
W	F	M	I	V	S	E	C	S	I	O	X	U	B	E
E	O	W	P	F	B	L	P	N	A	C	H	A	M	H
J	R	M	L	S	V	T	L	T	V	M	Q	R	A	C
X	D	S	M	Q	V	N	E	O	A	S	X	C	L	S
P	K	D	I	G	T	E	L	Y	R	D	X	T	W	R
S	S	S	Y	L	D	B	M	I	N	I	Y	R	B	O
O	M	N	E	C	R	P	R	F	S	H	K	O	K	P
O	O	W	U	R	O	T	E	L	O	R	V	E	H	C

BUGATTI   **PORSCHE**
FORD   **ROLLS ROYCE**
BMW   **MINI**
JAGUAR   **PEUGEOT**
CHEVROLET   **MASERATI**
LAMBORGHINI   **BENTLEY**

	6	2		9				
		7					1	9
			6	4		2		
	7	4			8			2
2	1			7			6	8
3			9			7	4	
		6		3	4			
1	4					8		
				5		9	7	

	3	8		1			7	2
	7		8	4				
			2	3				
				8		1	3	6
		5				9		
8	2	3		9				
				6	1			
				5	4		1	
1	9			2		3	5	

			2		9			1
	5			6	7		2	
	9	6				3		4
	4				6			7
		2		1		4		
9			8				3	
1		8				9	5	
	6		1	5			4	
5			6		2			

			8					
			4			5	2	
1		9			6	4	3	
	3			6		2		
7		2	1	3	8	5		6
		5		9			8	
	2	6	4			8		1
9	8			1				
			2					

1		3		9		2		
6				2	3		8	
							3	1
		2	9				4	
		1	5		2	8		
	3				4	5		
3	1							
	7		3	4				5
		9		8		4		3

S U D O K U

WINNERS in SPORT

1 Venus was the first out of the Williams sisters to win Wimbledon.

○ True   ○ False

2 Italy won the FIFA World Cup in 2006.

○ True   ○ False

3 England last won the Rugby World Cup in 2003.

○ True   ○ False

4 More pints were consumed in the 2014 Six Nations match England vs. Ireland than throughout the whole of Wimbledon 2017.

○ True   ○ False

5 More than 30,000kg of strawberries were consumed during Wimbledon 2017.

○ True   ○ False

True or False

6 Spain is home to the biggest football stadium in the world.

○ True   ○ False

7 The current World's Strongest Man, Eddie Hall, is the only man to have deadlifted 450kg under strongman rules.

○ True   ○ False

8 Cricket used the term 'home run' before baseball.

○ True   ○ False

9 Brazil is the only country to have played in every World Cup tournament.

○ True   ○ False

10 Usain Bolt has held the current world record for the men's 100-metre sprint since 2008.

○ True   ○ False

DOT TO DOT

GET THE TRAIN BACK ON THE TRACKS WITH THIS DOT TO DOT.

Roads

Which eight roads will get you from the centre of Wolverhampton to the centre of Grimsby the fastest?

A34	A19	M40
A61	A180	A5148
M18	A460	M5
A38	A52	A50
M1	A638	A47
A1033	A16	M6
A17	A5	A14

---- -- ---

-- --- ----

---- ---

Actors Who Never Won OSCARS® But Should Have

CLUES ON OPPOSITE PAGE!

CROSSWORD

Across:

3. Which actor starred alongside Richard Gere as the character Aaron Stampler in his debut film? (6,6)

7. Who broke off their engagement with Winona Ryder in 1993? (6,4)

9. Whose performance as Ripley in 1979 was their breakthrough role? (9,6)

10. Who had a role in *The Hunger Games*, *The Lost World* and *Crazy, Stupid, Love*? (8,5)

11. Who, prior to acting, was in a successful hip-hop duo with DJ Jazzy Jeff? (4,5)

Down:

1. Which actor shares his second name with a mythical bird possessing the ability to regenerate? (7,7)

2. Which actor known for playing a rogue pilot regularly flies himself between his New York City and Wyoming homes? (8,4)

4. Who played a villain with a penchant for spotted puppies? (5,5)

5. Who first became known after appearing on the television series *Welcome Back, Kotter* in the 1970s? (4,8)

6. Which 'scream queen' had her film debut in the 1978 horror *Halloween*? (5,3,6)

7. Which English actor appeared on the 1990 soap *Families*? (4,3)

8. Which actor had a role in the *Harry Potter* series as well as the 1994 film *Léon*? (4,6)

See if you can corral the names of the actors who starred in The Magnificent Seven.

1 ....

2 ....

3 ....

4 ....

5 ....

6 ....

7 ....

Smart SEQUENCE

RNMDJIEIHIX ....

BCIAKUTONR ....

JKACIWTHE ....

GVDOAHRLE ....

KIERASCHDTHRI ....

HATIAMNIDSR ....

TCLSAAAANRNOS ....

BIARAYNM ....

ROMAN & GREEK MYTHOLOGY

Trivia

1 In Greek mythology, who travelled to the land of the dead in order to find his wife?

....

2 Which musical instrument is the Greek god Pan associated with?

....

3 What is the Roman god equivalent to the Greek god Hermes?

....

4 In Roman mythology, there is an ancient god with no Greek equivalent. What is his name?

....

5 According to the ancient Greeks and Romans, there have been five Ages of Man. Which Age are we supposedly currently in?

....

6 Who is the Roman equivalent of the Greek goddess Demeter?

....

7 Who designed the labyrinth that held the Minotaur?

....

8 What was the name of the boy whose wings melted off as he flew too close to the sun?

....

9 Was Jupiter a leader of gods in Greek or Roman mythology?

....

10 Is it according to Greek or Roman mythology that Phaethon pulled his father's chariot too close to the sun, which scorched the ground, creating deserts?

....

11 Name the Gorgon who was destroyed by Perseus.

....

TRAVEL AROUND the WORLD
WORD SEARCH

M	H	B	K	X	G	A	L	A	P	A	G	O	S	L
S	U	E	M	P	W	E	T	A	J	M	A	H	A	L
E	F	R	U	M	P	A	I	G	X	U	N	Q	M	A
R	V	L	E	W	A	O	G	I	V	G	U	C	J	W
E	D	I	D	E	N	C	E	X	R	U	Q	X	A	T
N	I	N	E	Q	A	H	H	A	N	P	O	T	D	A
G	Z	W	J	M	M	X	N	U	K	Z	P	U	G	E
E	X	A	O	H	A	D	P	P	P	H	I	Q	H	R
T	M	L	W	A	C	D	P	V	O	I	E	D	J	G
I	E	L	E	A	A	E	E	I	S	L	C	E	Q	Y
I	E	L	N	J	N	G	C	R	P	R	K	C	Q	B
G	P	Y	Y	F	A	U	Q	I	T	N	E	H	H	N
A	O	K	A	A	L	C	K	U	N	O	G	G	U	U
N	D	N	X	O	V	O	L	P	Z	E	N	G	Q	T
Y	U	L	U	R	U	R	O	F	K	D	V	V	U	K

VENICE	GALÁPAGOS
SERENGETI	WAT PHO
TAJ MAHAL	NOTRE-DAME
MACHU PICCHU	GRAND CANYON
PANAMA CANAL	ULURU
GREAT WALL	BERLIN WALL

TYPES of CLOUD

Can you identify the cloud silhouettes with a little blue-sky thinking?

1

2

3

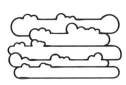

4

5

6

A. CUMULONIMBUS
B. CIRROCUMULUS
C. STRATUS

D. ALTOCUMULUS
E. STRATOCUMULUS
F. CUMULUS

Spot the DIFFERENCE

CAN YOU LOCATE THE DINER DEVELOPMENTS?

DOT TO DOT

Join up the dots to complete this remarkable ride!

SUPERB SUDOKU

EASY

8							1	
	1	5	3					7
	3	9	6					
		8	5		2			3
	7	9	3	1	6			
2			4		6	5		
					5	4	2	
9					7	1	3	
	2							9

EASY

	2			5	9			
	5			8	6	1		
		4	9	3			5	
9	8		6					
		1				8		
					7		2	5
	4		1	9	2			
	1	8	7				6	
	5	2					4	

MEDIUM

6	4			8			2	
		2		1	9	3		
5	1		9		6			
9			8					
8								2
				7				8
			3		5		6	9
	9	8	6			3		
	5			9			7	4

MEDIUM

3		2			4			5
					6		8	
	6			3	2			1
	9	7		1			4	6
			9					
1	3			2		7	9	
9			7	6			2	
	8		2					
7			8			3		9

HARD

	3					2	8	
7	8			2		4		
4			6				3	
		8	5	6				
5			8		2			3
			9	7	8			
	1			9				6
		3		7			9	4
		4	7			2		

HARD

3						5		
	7		2				1	4
		4				2		6
			7		2	4		
2		7	8	1	4	6		3
		5	6		3			
7		2				1		
4	1			6			3	
		3						5

1 Whoopi Goldberg created her stage name in part due to her fondness of flatulence.

○ True ○ False

2 Robert De Niro has a walk-in wardrobe he aptly named Christopher Walk-in, after his friend Christopher Walken.

○ True ○ False

3 OJ Simpson was put forward to play the Terminator.

○ True ○ False

4 In *Lord of the Rings: The Return of the King*, Elijah Wood used Alka-Seltzer tablets to foam at the mouth when Shelob stabs Frodo.

○ True ○ False

5 Forty squirrels were trained to crack nuts on a conveyor belt for Tim Burton's *Charlie and the Chocolate Factory*.

○ True ○ False

TRUE OR FALSE

6 David Fincher wrote the character of killer John Doe in *Se7en* for Kevin Spacey.

○ True ○ False

7 Charlie Sheen stayed awake for 48 hours to achieve a suitably wasted look for his cameo role in *Ferris Bueller's Day Off*.

○ True ○ False

8 Christian Bale based his character Patrick Bateman on Tom Cruise for *American Psycho*.

○ True ○ False

9 Leonardo DiCaprio is actually sketching a nude Kate Winslet in *Titanic*.

○ True ○ False

10 Something bad happens every time John Travolta's character is in the bathroom in *Pulp Fiction*.

○ True ○ False

 **You'll reach new levels of acclaim if you can name the world's highest peaks!**

1 ....

2 ....

3 ....

4 **Lhotse** ....

5 ....

6 ....

7 ....

8 ....

9 ....

10 ....

Smart SEQUENCE

Road Chat

LIVERPOOL to CARDIFF

Roads

Which eight roads will get you from the centre of Liverpool to the centre of Cardiff the fastest?

A570	M50	A43
M6	A40	A48
A38	A432	A5
M4	M5	A15
A666	A39	A470
A449	M42	A1
A59	A5080	M62

_ _ _ _ _   _ _ _   _ _

_ _   _ _ _   _ _ _

_ _   _ _ _ _

DC SUPERHEROES Word Scramble

IKHRAGLW ....

AAAUQNM ....

TEALFSHH ....

EOMNONRDWWA ....

PMEURSNA ....

SIREPULGR ....

MUEBEEBLB ....

AATBNM ....

Can you unjumble the
names of these caped crusaders?

PECULIAR PLACES

MATCHING GAME!

Countries	Places
UNITED STATES	DISAPPOINTMENT ISLANDS
UNITED STATES	BATMAN
TURKEY	CATBRAIN
ENGLAND	DEAD DOG BEACH
PUERTO RICO	BARBECUE
FRENCH POLYNESIA	DRAMA
GREECE	OGRE
CENTRAL LATVIA	ACCIDENT

Link these baffling place names to the countries they exist in!

WORLD CUP Winners

Trivia

1 In 1938, which nation became the first to win the World Cup for a second time?

....

2 The 1950 World Cup was the first to... ?

○ Not have a World Cup final
○ Feature an Asian nation
○ Be played in South America
○ Feature 16 competing nations

3 In 1978, Argentina became the fifth team to win the World Cup on home soil, who were the other four?

....

....

4 What year did England win the World Cup?

....

5 How often is the World Cup?

....

6 Who was the only nation to remain unbeaten throughout the 2010 World Cup?

....

7 For how many days did the Jules Rimet trophy famously go missing for before the World Cup in England?

....

8 Who scored a World Cup record of five goals in one game against Cameroon in USA 1994?

○ Hristo Stoichkov   ○ Oleg Salenko
○ Romário   ○ Roberto Baggio

9 Who was the only manager to win the FIFA World Cup twice?

○ Vicente Feola (Brazil)
○ Aimé Jacquet (France)
○ César Luis Menotti (Argentina)
○ Vittorio Pozzo (Italy)

10 Which teams have won two World Cups on the trot?

....

WORLD LEADERS

WORD SEARCH

I	N	E	L	S	O	N	M	A	N	D	E	L	A	B
P	R	A	M	A	L	I	A	L	A	D	U	O	B	V
E	Y	C	L	E	O	P	A	T	R	A	D	P	I	Z
A	K	N	L	A	Q	B	I	S	E	Q	J	W	U	Y
B	V	E	C	Q	W	O	G	E	N	E	K	E	R	V
C	G	E	L	R	L	C	R	A	F	O	N	A	O	J
F	I	H	D	N	A	G	E	L	P	W	C	F	J	S
J	U	L	I	U	S	C	A	E	S	A	R	Z	D	O
N	I	B	O	U	D	I	C	A	K	S	S	P	P	T
P	V	X	O	B	O	C	H	U	R	C	H	I	L	L
U	P	U	H	A	M	A	B	O	K	C	A	R	A	B
P	S	F	B	V	Z	B	C	Y	W	J	A	P	Z	O
G	M	D	O	N	A	L	D	T	R	U	M	P	P	I
K	V	Y	V	P	O	P	E	F	R	A	N	C	I	S
H	T	E	B	A	Z	I	L	E	N	E	E	U	Q	P

DONALD TRUMP
CHURCHILL
CLEOPATRA
GANDHI

JOAN OF ARC
DALAI LAMA
NELSON MANDELA
BARACK OBAMA

POPE FRANCIS
BOUDICA
QUEEN ELIZABETH
JULIUS CAESAR

DOT TO DOT

Join up the dots to complete these amazing metal men!

TYPES OF RED WINE

CLUES ON OPPOSITE PAGE!

CROSSWORD

Across:

2. Which wine made its way to California via The Gold Rush in the 1850s? (9)

6. Which wine is one of two parents to Cabernet Sauvignon, Carménère and Merlot? (8,5)

8. Which popular wine's name translates to 'young blackbird' in French? (6)

9. Which wine variety was originally named Côt? (6)

11. Which wine goes by numerous different names around the world including Tinto Fino, Tinta de Toro and Ull de Llebre? (11)

Down:

1. The name of this wine when translated from French means 'black pine cone'. (4,5)

3. Which wine was created in the 17th century in South West France through a chance crossing of Cabernet Franc and Sauvignon Blanc? (8,9)

4. Which wine's name closely translates to 'little green one' in French? (5,6)

5. Which Italian wine has a name deriving from the Latin sanguis Jovis, meaning 'the blood of Jove'? (10)

6. Which medium-bodied red wine was previously mistaken with Merlot and, before its true identity was discovered in Chile, was called Merlot Peumal? (9)

7. Which wine shares its name with a city in Iran, in the Fars Province, known for producing wine for the first time in history? (6)

10. Which light-bodied red wine, similar in taste to Pinot Noir, grows primarily in a region called Beaujolais? (5)

EASY

	8		9		1		7	
	6				8			4
		9	4					6
6			1		4			
	3		5	9	2		6	
			6		7			2
4					3	9		
5			8				4	
	9		7		6		3	

EASY

2	8	6						
1							7	8
5			8	2				9
9		2			4	6		
			6		7			
		8	5			1		7
3				4	5			1
7	1							6
						7	5	3

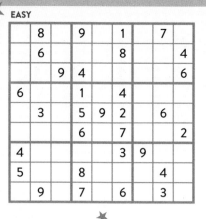

MEDIUM

6		7	4				8	
	1				5	2	7	
	9					1		6
	6		9		1	7		
				3				
		9	6		2		1	
1		6					2	
	3	5	7				6	
	7				6	9		5

MEDIUM

		3					7	
4				3	5	6		
2	7		8				3	4
9				4			2	
			6		1			
	8			2				9
5	3				4		8	6
		7	9	8				3
	6					9		

HARD

		1	2	9		6	3	
		7	6		8		2	
		2			4			5
	5							3
		6				9		
8							4	
6			4			3		
	9		7		1	2		
	2	5		6	3	4		

HARD

1			2			4		
	7						5	
5				8			6	3
			9	1			8	4
		1	8		3	5		
8	6			2	5			
4	7			9				5
	2					7		
		8			4			9

SUDOKU Superstar

Word Scramble
CRIME AUTHORS

HSTRAECGIHAATI ....

LTNLEUDREHR ....

JERSEMANAPOSTT ....

SESGIARTLOSN ....

HJONLREACRÉ ....

PETNEKGNISH ....

ANIANRINK ....

ECEIDLLH ....

Spot the DIFFERENCE

It's a marvel that not everyone knows the Seven Wonders of the Ancient World. Do you?

1 ....

2 ....

3 ....

4 ....

5 ....

6 ....

7 ....

Smart SEQUENCE

ROMAN GODS

WORD SEARCH

M	H	Y	N	E	M	E	S	I	S	K	D	S	M	R
G	D	B	G	S	Y	J	I	U	L	G	H	D	Z	Q
L	D	W	Q	K	I	U	O	H	H	E	E	D	D	U
A	V	R	E	N	I	M	H	B	P	C	R	L	K	E
G	Z	N	U	G	I	N	R	Z	U	W	C	I	R	I
M	S	G	R	F	G	L	A	P	H	B	U	A	G	L
Q	A	G	E	S	G	P	I	C	M	C	L	I	B	O
L	T	R	N	B	D	D	T	V	L	I	E	R	D	Z
L	T	O	S	Y	F	X	D	I	T	U	S	I	E	Z
C	F	V	L	A	O	W	O	Z	R	X	V	S	R	Y
V	T	X	U	L	C	T	I	E	L	M	E	F	D	Y
Q	F	N	A	N	O	L	Q	I	T	R	G	K	Q	A
B	A	S	Q	G	D	P	J	T	E	I	S	C	A	Z
N	E	P	T	U	N	E	A	C	X	O	G	A	A	D
C	L	N	S	C	V	C	O	B	B	O	C	I	E	C

CUPID	HERCULES	FAUNA
MARS	VULCAN	IRIS
APOLLO	MINERVA	NEMESIS
NEPTUNE	BACCHUS	CERES

Random RECORD BREAKERS

1 The largest rubber-band ball is made up of 600,000 elastic bands.

  ○ True   ○ False

2 The former American football player Troy Polamalu had his hair insured by Head & Shoulders for $1 million.

  ○ True   ○ False

3 The world's tallest man is 251cm tall.

  ○ True   ○ False

4 The world's tallest dog is as tall as the average female lion.

  ○ True   ○ False

5 'Red lorry, yellow lorry' is the world's hardest tongue-twister.

  ○ True   ○ False

TRUE OR FALSE

6 Donald A. Gorske is famous for consuming 26,000 Big Macs within his lifetime.

○ True   ○ False

7 Georges Christen is famous for having the largest bobble-head collection.

○ True   ○ False

8 The longest moustache recorded was 4.29 metres long.

○ True   ○ False

9 The largest swimsuit photo shoot consisted of over 1,000 bikini-clad women.

○ True   ○ False

10 The biggest barbeque in the world saw over 28,000 kilos of beef being grilled.

○ True   ○ False

CAN YOU LOCATE THE VARIATIONS ON THIS VACATION?

Best Britsh ALES

CLUES ON OPPOSITE PAGE!

CROSSWORD

Across:

4. Which brewery based in Lewes distributes Sussex Best Bitter? (7)

5. Which ale is named after the term for difficult conditions in the sport of cricket? (6,6)

7. Which ale is named after a holy man's appendage? (7,6)

8. Which Kentish ale was first brewed to commemorate the Battle of Britain? (8)

9. Which ale is named after a sandbank situated in Cornwall at the mouth of the estuary of the River Camel? (4,3)

10. Which ale could also be described as an elderly sneaky chicken? (3,6,3)

11. Which ale, brewed next to the river Thames, is Fuller's Brewery's leading product? (6,5)

12. Which ale first brewed in 1979 is now owned by Greene King Brewery? (3,8,3)

Down:

1. What is often referred to as the 'spice of beer' and has been used in beer-making for 1,000 years? (4)

2. Which ale's name is derived from the fact that the drink was so popular with British troops stationed in India in the 19th century? (3)

3. Which traditional Newcastle ale is now brewed by Heineken? (9,5,3)

6. This ale shares its name with a mischievous spirit? (9)

ROCK MUSIC

Trivia

1 For which album did Oasis win the Brit Award for Brit Album of 30 Years?

....

2 Since the release of Led Zeppelin's *IV*, how many copies have been sold?

- ○ 23 million
- ○ 17 million
- ○ 1 million
- ○ 750,000

3 The hit single 'Desert Rose' was sung by which famous artist?

....

4 Elvis Presley is known as the 'King of Rock and Roll'. From which Elvis song do these lyrics come from?

'You know I can be found, sitting home all alone, If you can't come around, at least please telephone.'

....

5 What is the real name of The Beatles' drummer?

....

6 Who of the following were **NOT** in Led Zeppelin?

○ Jimmy Page ○ John Entwistle
○ John Paul Jones ○ John Bonham

7 How many official members of The Beatles were there?

....

8 Who is famous for burning his guitar?

....

9 Whose guitar looked like a black-and-white bullseye?

....

10 What honour did Bowie turn down in 2003?

....

11 Who threw the party where Bowie and John Lennon first met?

....

WHITE WINE Word Scramble

ARDANCOYNH ....

OIIPROTGNGI ....

VEENTRNOIM ....

NIPTDPEELCOIUP ....

NNBHECCINLA ....

JRAHTIOIEW ....

CSTMAU ....

SLINRGEI ....

Can you unjumble the names of these tasty tipples?

CAPITAL CITIES

WORD SEARCH *of the World*

A	R	R	E	B	N	A	C	K	K	U	J	W	J	I
M	E	S	W	E	X	U	A	W	L	I	E	D	G	C
N	H	F	B	N	M	T	M	W	H	L	O	P	B	M
T	I	W	S	A	H	R	I	F	L	R	I	I	Q	R
J	U	L	N	M	N	E	L	I	Y	E	B	Q	B	O
W	U	I	A	G	J	G	N	I	W	Y	A	C	K	X
Q	L	N	T	J	W	G	K	Z	M	K	H	M	F	L
A	D	N	D	N	T	W	A	O	N	J	D	U	N	K
U	V	S	N	O	S	B	M	C	K	A	U	S	J	A
G	M	E	N	I	T	X	P	O	L	V	B	C	U	J
J	V	J	P	L	M	E	A	T	K	I	A	A	U	X
H	S	Z	L	T	J	F	L	I	S	K	U	T	T	J
S	F	Z	T	S	R	X	A	U	I	Q	P	P	P	J
M	P	K	L	U	O	E	S	Q	T	R	Y	U	O	D
I	O	P	B	X	V	L	R	Q	V	R	Q	G	T	R

ABU DHABI   KAMPALA

BANGKOK   LIMA

CANBERRA   REYKJAVIK

KATHMANDU   WELLINGTON

SEOUL   MUSCAT

QUITO   MANILA

POP BANDS

CLUES ON OPPOSITE PAGE!

CROSSWORD

Across:

3. Which American rock and pop band's name is inspired by cheeky primates? (3,7)

7. Which English rock group were originally called the New Yardbirds? (3,8)

8. Which band did the three Gibb brothers form? (3,4)

10. Which Motown band had the no. 1 hit 'I Can't Help Myself (Sugar Pie, Honey Bunch)' in June 1965? (4,4)

11. Which group did Jackie and Marlon form along with their other siblings? (7,4)

12. Which group was Veronica Bennett the lead singer of? (3,8)

Down:

1. Which band released 'You Really Got Me' as their third single? (3,5)

2. Diana Ross fronted which 1960s Motown band? (3,8)

4. Which band's last album of the 1960s was named *Tommy*? (3,3)

5. Which band was Steve Marriott originally part of before leaving to form Humble Pie? (3,5,5)

6. Which English rock band were formed in Liverpool in 1960? (3,7)

9. Which band were known for their surf songs and vocal harmonies? (5,4)

Spot the DIFFERENCE

CAN YOU FIND THE SWITCHES IN THIS SITUATION?

ROCK 'N' ROLL

1 Ryan Adams and Bryan Adams share the same birthday.

○ True ○ False

2 Freddie Mercury once dressed Princess Diana up in drag.

○ True ○ False

3 Aerosmith earned more from Guitar Hero than their albums.

○ True ○ False

4 The Ramones have sold more T-shirts than albums.

○ True ○ False

5 Drew Barrymore's uncle, Chip Taylor, wrote the song 'Wild Thing'.

○ True ○ False

True OR False

6 Bob Dylan's real name is Elston Gunn.

○ True ○ False

7 Vinnie Vincent wrote the soundtracks for *Happy Days* and *Joanie Loves Chachi* before he joined KISS.

○ True ○ False

8 Pink Floyd has never made it into the American Rock and Roll Hall of Fame.

○ True ○ False

9 Rock and Roll is a form of rock music developed in the 1950s and 1960s.

○ True ○ False

10 The Beatles are the only act to have knocked themselves off the top of the chart with 'She Loves You' and 'I Want to Hold Your Hand'.

○ True ○ False

EASY

	3				7			
7		5	4	8				
			7	1			2	5
4			2			1		
5		9		3		8		2
		2			7			4
3	8		1	9				
				6	2	3		7
		6					8	

EASY

4		3	9	1			8	
5	6	1			7			
			5		2			
		4		2			3	
	3						2	
	5			6		7		
		1		5				
		2				3	6	9
	7			9	4	1		2

MEDIUM

9	2		4			7		6
	4		7			3		
7			9		8			
3		4	2					1
8					3	4		2
			1		9			3
		3			4		9	
4		5			6		1	7

MEDIUM

				9	4			
1	3	8	5		6			
	2				3			5
		3	8			9		2
		3	4	2				
2		5			1	3		
8			6				2	
		4		5	8	6	9	
		2	3					

HARD

	4	1			6			8
5					1		2	
		2		7				
4		5	3			9		
	3	7		9		1	5	
		9			4	2		3
				8		7		
	7		4					9
9			7			4	6	

HARD

	4		7					
		2	4		6	3		9
9			1		2			8
		9			3			4
	2						3	
3			8			9		
7			3		4			2
2		8	6		5	4		
					7		5	

MYTHICAL BEASTS

WORD SEARCH

V	T	H	X	S	H	K	S	R	N	L	D	C	C	P
V	F	T	L	X	Z	G	F	L	Y	P	R	A	H	G
B	L	C	Y	C	L	O	P	S	J	Y	T	D	F	D
I	R	E	E	E	H	S	N	A	B	Y	M	U	W	A
Z	L	B	P	S	S	E	C	W	S	I	D	I	R	D
A	F	W	S	R	Q	F	V	E	N	F	T	D	G	C
K	N	P	Y	J	E	A	X	O	F	J	Y	F	P	E
V	U	T	Z	H	A	C	T	U	N	H	R	J	H	N
S	N	O	X	X	I	A	H	W	C	V	H	W	O	T
S	I	O	X	O	U	G	F	A	C	Z	C	V	E	A
X	C	F	N	R	X	T	S	L	U	V	H	Z	N	U
U	O	G	I	P	P	R	T	R	F	N	Z	X	I	R
B	R	I	H	J	G	S	N	C	G	H	O	Q	X	E
D	N	B	P	G	F	Q	J	N	I	F	F	I	R	G
G	F	W	S	N	U	B	C	Y	C	Q	R	L	A	Y

UNICORN　　**BANSHEE**
BIGFOOT　　**CYCLOPS**
CENTAUR　　**PHOENIX**
HYDRA　　**GRIFFIN**
MINOTAUR　　**HARPY**
SPHINX　　**LEPRECHAUN**

Solutions
NO CHEATING!

4 **RAF SILHOUETTES**
1. Avro Vulcan 2. Tornado GR4 3. Hawker Hurricane 4. Avro Lancaster
5. Handley Page Halifax 6. Supermarine Spitfire 7. Eurofighter Typhoon
8. Lockheed C-130 Hercules 9. Avro Lincoln

5 **CAR PARTS WORD SEARCH**

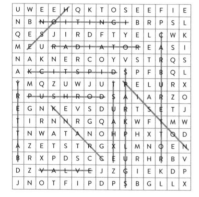

6 **WHICH LIGHT TO WHICH BATTERY?**

LIGHT	1	2	3	4
BATTERY	C	B	A	D

8 **MATCH THESE CAPITALS**

Lithuania – Vilnius.
Rep. of Congo – Brazzaville.
Turkmenistan – Ashgabat.
Estonia – Tallinn. Gabon – Libreville.
Tajikistan – Dushanbe.
Paraguay – Asunción. Ecuador – Quito.
Which capital city is this – Sofia.

9 **SENSATIONAL SUDOKU**

"You can find the solutions for the medium and hard puzzles on the oppostite page."

2	5	3	8	9	4	1	7	6
1	9	6	2	3	7	5	8	4
8	7	4	1	5	6	9	2	3
3	8	1	9	4	2	6	5	7
9	6	7	3	8	5	4	1	2
4	2	5	7	6	1	8	3	9
6	1	9	5	2	3	7	4	8
7	3	8	4	1	9	2	6	5
5	4	2	6	7	8	3	9	1

EASY

6	3	7	9	5	1	5	2	4
8	5	4	3	6	2	9	1	7
9	2	1	4	8	7	6	3	5
1	9	3	7	4	8	5	6	2
5	8	2	6	9	3	7	4	1
7	4	6	2	1	5	3	8	9
3	6	9	5	2	4	1	7	8
2	1	5	8	7	6	4	9	3
4	7	8	1	3	9	2	5	6

EASY

5	1	4	7	2	3	6	8	9
9	2	6	5	8	4	1	7	3
8	7	3	1	9	6	5	2	4
6	9	7	4	1	5	2	3	8
2	3	1	6	7	8	9	4	5
4	5	8	9	3	2	7	6	1
1	6	9	3	4	7	8	5	2
3	8	5	2	6	9	4	1	7
7	4	2	8	5	1	3	9	6

MEDIUM

9	4	6	1	8	2	7	5	3
3	1	8	5	9	7	4	2	6
2	7	5	6	4	3	8	9	1
4	9	2	3	1	8	5	6	7
6	3	7	2	5	4	9	1	8
8	5	1	7	6	9	2	3	4
1	2	4	8	3	5	6	7	9
7	8	3	9	2	6	1	4	5
5	6	9	4	7	1	3	8	2

HARD

9	4	6	5	1	2	8	7	3
7	2	8	4	6	3	5	1	9
1	3	5	8	7	9	4	6	2
5	8	4	6	9	7	2	3	1
3	7	2	1	8	4	6	9	5
6	1	9	2	3	5	7	4	8
2	5	7	3	4	1	9	8	6
8	9	3	7	2	6	1	5	4
4	6	1	9	5	8	3	2	7

HARD

10 SPOT THE DIFFERENCE

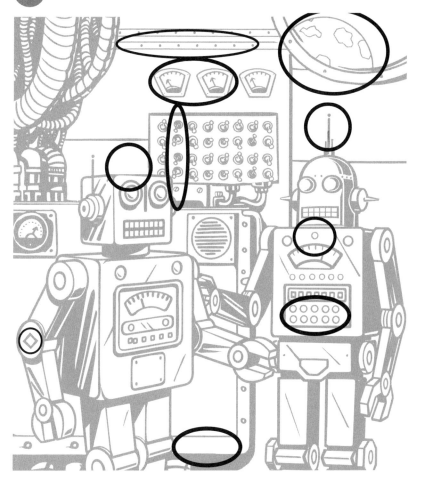

12 VOLCANOES WORD SCRAMBLE

1. Mount Etna 2. Mount Fuji 3. Krakatoa 4. Mount St. Helens
5. Mount Vesuvius 6. Mount Olympus 7. Mount Pinatubo 8. Mount Tambora

13 BIRDS OF THE WORLD WORD SEARCH

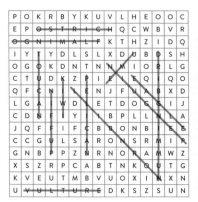

14 POISONOUS ANIMALS OF THE WORLD CROSSWORD

16 MATCH THAT HAT SILHOUETTES

1. Bobble hat 2. Beret 3. Trilby
4. Bowler 5. Pork pie hat
6. Panama 7. Fedora 8. Flat cap
8. Top hat

17 LEICESTER TO CANTERBURY ROAD CHAT

A47, A5460, M1, M25,
A282, A2, M2, A2, A2050

18 MIND-BENDING QUESTIONS TRIVIA

1. There's a hole in it. 2. No one, they are his sisters. 3. The letter 't'. 4. Thursday.
5. Three, as the boat floats. 6. Susan. 7. He's walking. 8. A stamp. 9. Monaco.
10. One, the rest are anniversaries. 11. A peacock doesn't lay eggs, a peahen does.

20 BOND FILMS SMART SEQUENCE

1. Dr. No 2. From Russia with Love 3. Goldfinger 4. Thunderball 5. Casino Royale 6. You Only Live Twice 7. On Her Majesty's Secret Service 8. Diamonds Are Forever 9. Live and Let Die 10. The Man with the Golden Gun 11. The Spy Who Loved Me 12. Moonraker 13. For Your Eyes Only 14. Octopussy 15. Never Say Never Again 16. A View to a Kill 17. The Living Daylights 18. Licence to Kill 19. GoldenEye 20. Tomorrow Never Dies 21. The World Is Not Enough 22. Die Another Day 23. Casino Royale 24. Quantum of Solace 25. Skyfall 26. Spectre

22 SPACE TRAVEL TRUE OR FALSE

1. True. 2. False. Only astronauts who landed on the moon were placed in quarantine. 3. True. Venus is the hottest planet. 4. True. There is no wind on the Moon to erode them. 5. False. 6. True. 7. False. He was the second man to walk on the Moon. 8. False. The flag was blasted away upon departure. 9. True. Astronauts experience less time when in space. 10. True.

24 PLACES OF THE WORLD WORD SCRAMBLE

1. Great Barrier Reef
2. Machu Picchu
3. Serengeti
4. Grand Canyon
5. Victoria Falls
6. Amazon River
7. Yellowstone
8. Pyramids of Giza 9. Taj Mahal

25 SUPER SUDOKU CHALLENGE

EASY

3	1	2	5	9	8	6	7	4
5	9	4	7	6	3	1	8	2
7	6	8	4	2	1	3	5	9
4	2	1	9	3	5	8	6	7
8	7	9	1	4	6	2	3	5
6	3	5	8	7	2	9	4	1
2	4	7	3	8	9	5	1	6
1	8	6	2	5	7	4	9	3
9	5	3	6	1	4	7	2	8

EASY

8	4	5	7	9	6	1	2	3
7	9	6	3	2	1	5	8	4
3	2	1	4	5	8	6	7	9
6	1	3	8	7	5	9	4	2
9	8	4	6	3	2	7	1	5
2	5	7	9	1	4	3	6	8
5	3	8	1	4	7	2	9	6
4	7	9	2	6	3	8	5	1
1	6	2	5	8	9	4	3	7

MEDIUM

4	1	2	8	5	3	9	6	7
6	7	3	2	1	9	4	5	8
9	8	5	4	7	6	1	3	2
5	3	8	6	4	2	7	1	9
2	9	7	5	8	1	6	4	3
1	6	4	3	9	7	8	2	5
3	4	9	7	6	5	2	8	1
8	2	1	9	3	4	5	7	6
7	5	6	1	2	8	3	9	4

HARD

4	7	3	5	2	1	6	9	8
5	9	2	6	8	4	7	1	3
8	1	6	9	3	7	4	5	2
7	3	4	1	5	8	2	6	9
1	2	5	4	6	9	3	8	7
6	8	9	3	7	2	5	4	1
2	6	7	8	1	5	9	3	4
9	5	8	7	4	3	1	2	6
3	4	1	2	9	6	8	7	5

HARD

6	2	9	3	7	8	4	5	1
8	1	4	6	2	5	3	9	7
5	7	3	9	4	1	6	8	2
3	9	5	4	6	7	1	2	8
7	8	6	2	1	3	5	4	9
2	4	1	5	8	9	7	6	3
9	3	8	7	5	6	2	1	4
1	6	2	8	3	4	9	7	5
4	5	7	1	9	2	8	3	6

28 **TIME LORD SMART SEQUENCE**

1. William Hartnell 2. Patrick Troughton
3. Jon Pertwee 4. Tom Baker

5. Peter Davison 6. Colin Baker
7. Sylvester McCoy 8. Paul McGann
9. Christopher Eccleston
10. David Tennant 11. Matt Smith
12. Peter Capaldi 13. Jodie Whittaker

29 SWINDON TO BRIGHTON ROAD CHAT

A419, M4, A34, A339, M25, A23, A27, A4259

30 STAR CONSTELLATIONS CROSSWORD

32 HISTORIC DATES TRUE OR FALSE

1. True. 2. True. 3. False. It was abolished in 1981. 4. False. The Nintendo 64 was first sold 4 years after. 5. True. 6. True. Prohibition ended in 1933. 7. False. The iPod was introduced 3 years before. 8. True. 9. False. Pluto was reclassified as a dwarf in 2006, 4 years after Brazil last won the World Cup. 10. False. It took 80 years.

34 CARPENTRY JOINTS MATCHING GAME

1. Rabbet joint
2. Tongue and dado joint
3. Dado rabbet joint
4. Butt joint
5. Lap joint
6. Through dado joint
7. Mitre joint
8. Dovetail joint
9. Half cross lap joint

35 BEERS OF THE WORLD WORD SEARCH

BRAHMA, SKOL, CORONA, HEINEKEN, BUDWEISER, GUINNESS

36 ASHES TRIVIA

1. Leg By 2. Darren Gough
3. Bill Woodfull 4. Mark Waugh
5. None 6. Andy Caddick
7. One 8. Every 2 years 9. 1882-83
10. Wally Hammond 11. Andrew

38 SUDOKU

EASY

1	8	4	2	9	7	5	6	3
5	7	6	3	1	4	9	2	8
9	3	2	6	8	5	4	7	1
7	4	5	9	3	1	2	8	6
8	6	3	5	4	2	1	9	7
2	1	9	8	7	6	3	4	5
4	2	7	1	6	3	8	5	9
3	5	8	7	2	9	6	1	4
6	9	1	4	5	8	7	3	2

EASY

8	2	7	6	4	5	1	9	3
9	1	6	7	3	2	4	5	8
3	4	5	9	1	8	2	7	6
1	8	3	5	2	4	7	6	9
2	5	9	1	7	6	8	3	4
7	6	4	3	8	9	5	2	1
4	3	8	2	6	7	9	1	5
6	9	2	8	5	1	3	4	7
5	7	1	4	9	3	6	8	2

MEDIUM

1	6	7	2	9	8	4	5	3
3	8	4	7	5	1	6	2	9
9	2	5	6	3	4	7	1	8
2	5	1	9	6	7	8	3	4
6	4	3	5	8	2	9	7	1
7	9	8	4	1	3	5	6	2
5	1	6	3	4	9	2	8	7
4	3	2	8	7	5	1	9	6
8	7	9	1	2	6	3	4	5

MEDIUM

5	4	6	7	2	3	1	9	8
8	1	3	6	9	4	5	2	7
9	7	2	5	1	8	6	4	3
6	5	7	1	3	2	4	8	9
2	8	1	4	7	9	3	5	6
3	9	4	8	5	6	7	1	2
7	6	5	9	8	1	2	3	4
4	2	8	3	6	5	9	7	1
1	3	9	2	4	7	8	6	5

HARD

5	1	8	2	7	9	4	3	6
4	7	2	6	3	5	9	8	1
3	6	9	8	4	1	7	2	5
6	9	4	7	1	2	3	5	8
2	8	5	3	6	4	1	7	9
7	3	1	9	5	8	2	6	4
8	2	6	1	9	3	5	4	7
1	4	3	5	8	7	6	9	2
9	5	7	4	2	6	8	1	3

HARD

4	6	8	9	7	2	3	5	1
9	1	5	3	6	8	4	2	7
7	2	3	4	1	5	9	8	6
1	4	7	6	2	9	5	3	8
2	3	6	5	8	1	7	9	4
8	5	9	7	3	4	1	6	2
6	8	4	1	9	3	2	7	5
3	7	1	2	5	6	8	4	9
5	9	2	8	4	7	6	1	3

39 LAND'S END TO JOHN O'GROATS ROAD CHAT

A30, M5, M6, A74, M73, M80, M9, A99

40 NAME THAT COUNTRY SILHOUETTES

1. Colombia **2.** Mexico **3.** Venezuela
4. Philippines **5.** Thailand **6.** Denmark
7. Brazil **8.** Norway **9.** Ireland

41 WORLD'S FASTEST RUNNERS WORD SCRAMBLE

1. Usain Bolt **2.** Jesse Owens
3. Justin Gatlin **4.** Tommie
Smith **5.** Maurice Greene
6. Donovan Bailey **7.** Carl
Lewis **8.** Tyson Gay

42 OSCAR WINNERS SMART SEQUENCE

1. Casey Affleck **2.** Leonardo DiCaprio
3. Eddie Redmayne **4.** Matthew
McConaughey **5.** Daniel Day-Lewis
6. Jean Dujardin **7.** Colin Firth
8. Jeff Bridges **9.** Sean Penn
10. Daniel Day-Lewis **11.** Forest
Whitaker **12.** Philip Seymour Hoffman
13. Jamie Foxx **14.** Sean Penn
15. Adrien Brody **16.** Denzel
Washington **17.** Russell Crowe

43 SUBERB SUDOKU PUZZLES

6	8	7	2	4	9	3	5	1
1	4	2	7	3	5	9	6	8
5	3	9	6	8	1	2	7	4
7	5	3	4	1	6	8	9	2
8	2	1	9	7	3	6	4	5
4	9	6	5	2	8	7	1	3
2	1	5	3	6	7	4	8	9
3	7	8	1	9	4	5	2	6
9	6	4	8	5	2	1	3	7

EASY

6	7	8	2	4	1	3	9	5
4	1	3	8	5	9	6	2	7
5	2	9	7	3	6	4	1	8
2	5	4	9	8	3	1	7	6
9	3	6	1	7	4	8	5	2
7	8	1	5	6	2	9	3	4
1	9	7	4	2	8	5	6	3
3	4	2	6	9	5	7	8	1
8	6	5	3	1	7	2	4	9

EASY

4	8	6	5	3	1	9	2	7
5	3	1	9	2	7	6	4	8
9	7	2	8	4	6	1	3	5
8	5	4	1	7	9	3	6	2
1	2	9	3	6	5	8	7	4
3	6	7	2	8	4	5	1	9
2	9	3	7	1	8	4	5	6
6	1	5	4	9	2	7	8	3
7	4	8	6	5	3	2	9	1

MEDIUM

7	1	5	9	6	3	8	4	2
6	8	2	5	4	7	3	9	1
4	9	3	1	2	8	5	7	6
9	6	4	8	1	5	7	2	3
2	5	7	4	3	9	6	1	8
1	3	8	2	7	6	9	4	5
5	2	9	3	8	1	4	6	7
8	7	1	6	9	4	2	3	5
3	4	6	7	5	2	1	8	9

MEDIUM

5	8	7	4	2	1	9	3	6
2	9	6	3	7	5	4	1	8
1	4	3	6	8	9	5	2	7
7	1	4	8	6	3	2	5	9
8	3	2	9	5	7	6	4	1
6	5	9	1	4	2	7	8	3
3	6	1	5	9	4	8	7	2
9	2	5	7	1	8	3	6	4
4	7	8	2	3	6	1	9	5

HARD

9	1	3	7	5	8	6	4	2
7	4	5	9	6	2	3	8	1
2	6	8	4	1	3	5	7	9
6	5	9	2	8	1	4	3	7
4	8	7	5	3	9	2	1	6
3	2	1	6	7	4	8	9	5
5	3	4	1	2	7	9	6	8
8	7	2	3	9	6	1	5	4
1	9	6	8	4	5	7	2	3

HARD

44 EXPLORERS WORD SEARCH

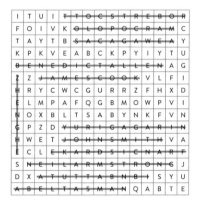

47 HISTORY OF DANCE CROSSWORD

48 STRANGE TRADITIONS TRUE OR FALSE

1. True. 2. True. 3. True. 4. True. 5. True. 6. False. 7. True. It is thought to bring good luck. 8. False. 9. True. To celebrate fertility. 10. True. At 30 pepper is thrown.

50 BODMIN TO STROUD ROAD CHAT

A30, M5, A419, A46

51 GREEK PHILOSOPHERS WORD SCRAMBLE

1. Plato 2. Aristotle 3. Pythagoras
4. Archimedes 5. Socrates 6. Atticus
7. Empedocles 8. Thales

52 SPOT THE DIFFERENCE

54 NATURE'S FASTEST AND SLOWEST TRIVA

1. Seahorse 2. Starfish
3. Snail 4. 68mph
5. Sailfish 6. 75mph
7. Greyhound 8. Manatee
9. Peregrine falcon
10. Lion 11. Grizzly bear
12. Giant tortoise

56 OLYMPICS 100M SMART SEQUENCE

1. Usain Bolt 2. Usain Bolt
3. Usain Bolt 4. Justin
Gatlin 5. Maurice Greene
6. Donovan Bailey
7. Linford Christie
8. Carl Lewis 9. Carl Lewis
10. Allan Wells

57 WHO SAID WHAT MATCHING GAME

1. Albert Einstein
2. Leon Trotsky
3. Yoda
4. Socrates
5. Gandi
6. Benjamin Franklin
7. Donald trump
8. Mark Twain
9. Homer Simpson
10. Winston Churchill

58 CARS WORD SEARCH

D	N	Q	I	U	X	Z	I	T	L	N	L	G	I	O
M	I	J	S	P	V	Q	G	Y	Z	O	E	Q	N	D
E	T	F	I	S	B	F	D	L	L	P	I	D	I	C
Y	C	O	I	T	T	A	G	U	B	H	T	E	H	R
N	E	Y	E	C	A	Y	H	R	Z	Y	E	I	G	C
T	R	P	O	G	N	R	H	A	O	R	Y	A	R	I
F	K	B	G	R	U	Y	E	Y	F	P	A	G	O	J
W	F	M	I	V	S	E	C	S	I	O	X	U	B	E
E	O	W	P	F	B	P	N	A	C	H	A	M	H	M
J	R	M	L	S	V	I	T	V	M	Q	R	A	C	I
X	D	S	M	Q	V	N	E	O	A	S	X	C	L	S
P	K	D	I	G	T	E	L	Y	R	D	X	T	W	R
S	S	S	Y	L	D	B	M	I	N	I	Y	R	B	O
O	M	N	E	C	R	P	R	F	S	H	K	O	K	P
O	O	W	U	R	O	T	E	L	O	R	V	E	H	C

59 SUDOKU

5	6	2	3	9	1	4	8	7
4	3	7	2	8	5	6	1	9
9	8	1	6	4	7	2	5	3
6	7	4	5	1	8	3	9	2
2	1	9	4	7	3	5	6	8
3	5	8	9	6	2	7	4	1
7	9	6	8	3	4	1	2	5
1	4	5	7	2	9	8	3	6
8	2	3	1	5	6	9	7	4

EASY

9	3	8	6	1	5	4	7	2
2	7	1	8	4	9	5	6	3
5	6	4	2	3	7	8	9	1
7	4	9	5	8	2	1	3	6
6	1	5	4	7	3	9	2	8
8	2	3	1	9	6	7	4	5
4	5	7	3	6	1	2	8	9
3	8	2	9	5	4	6	1	7
1	9	6	7	2	8	3	5	4

EASY

7	8	3	2	4	9	5	6	1
4	5	1	3	6	7	8	2	9
2	9	6	5	8	1	3	7	4
8	4	5	9	3	6	2	1	7
6	3	2	7	1	5	4	9	8
9	1	7	8	2	4	6	3	5
1	2	8	4	7	3	9	5	6
3	6	9	1	5	8	7	4	2
5	7	4	6	9	2	1	8	3

MEDIUM

2	4	3	9	8	5	6	1	7
6	7	8	3	4	1	9	5	2
1	5	9	2	7	6	4	3	8
8	3	1	5	6	4	2	7	9
7	9	2	1	3	8	5	4	6
4	6	5	7	9	2	1	8	3
3	2	6	4	5	7	8	9	1
9	8	4	6	1	3	7	2	5
5	1	7	8	2	9	3	6	4

HARD

1	8	3	4	9	7	2	5	6
6	9	5	1	2	3	7	8	4
4	2	7	8	5	6	9	3	1
5	6	2	9	1	8	3	4	7
7	4	1	5	3	2	8	6	9
9	3	8	7	6	4	5	1	2
3	1	4	2	7	5	6	9	8
8	7	6	3	4	9	1	2	5
2	5	9	6	8	1	4	7	3

HARD

60 WINNERS IN SPORT TRUE OR FALSE

1. True. 2. True. 3. True. 4. True. 160,547 pints of beer were sold. 5. True. An estimated 34,000kg of strawberries were consumed. 6. False. The largest stadium in the world belongs to North Korea. 7. False. He is the only man to have deadlifted 500kg. 8. False. 9. True. 10. False. Bolt has held the current record since 2009 after beating his previous 2008 record.

63 WOLVERHAMPTON TO GRIMSBY ROAD CHAT

A460, M6, A38, M1, M18, M180, A180, A16

64 ACTORS WHO NEVER WON OSCARS® BUT SHOULD HAVE CROSSWORD

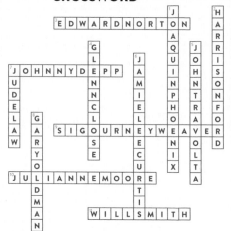

66 MAGNIFICENT SEVEN SMART SEQUENCE

1. Yul Brynner 2. Steve McQueen 3. Charles Bronson 4. Robert Vaughn 5. Brad Dexter 6. James Coburn 7. Horst Buchholz

67 LEAD GUITARISTS WORD SCRAMBLE

1. Jimi Hendrix 2. Kurt Cobain 3. Jack White 4. Dave Grohl 5. Keith Richards 6. Adrian Smith 7. Carlos Santana 8. Brian May

68 ROMAN AND GREEK MYTHOLOGY TRIVIA

1. Orpheus 2. Pipes 3. Mercury 4. Janus 5. Iron 6. Ceres 7. Daedalus 8. Icarus 9. Roman 10. Greek 11. Medusa

70 TRAVEL THE WORLD WORD SEARCH

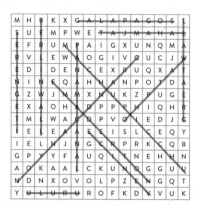

71 TYPES OF CLOUD MATCHING GAME

1. Cirrocumulus 2. Cumulonimbus 3. Altocumulus 4. Stratocumulus 5. Stratus 6. Cumulus

72 SPOT THE DIFFERENCE

76 ACTORS TRUE OR FALSE

1. True. 2. False. 3. True. 4. True. 5. True. 6. False. 7. True. 8. True. 9. False. It is director James Cameron who is actually doing the sketching. 10. True.

78 HIGHEST MOUNTAINS SMART SEQUENCE

1. Mount Everest 2. K2
3. Kangchenjunga 4. Lhotse
5. Makalu 6. Cho Oyu
7. Dhaulagiri I 8. Manaslu
9. Nanga Parbat
10. Gasherbrum I

75 SUBERB SUDOKU PUZZLES

8	4	2	7	5	9	3	1	6
6	1	5	3	2	4	8	9	7
7	3	9	6	1	8	2	5	4
1	6	8	5	7	2	9	4	3
4	5	7	9	3	1	6	8	2
2	9	3	4	8	6	5	7	1
3	7	6	1	9	5	4	2	8
9	8	4	2	6	7	1	3	5
5	2	1	8	4	3	7	6	9

EASY

8	2	7	1	6	5	9	3	4
3	5	9	4	7	8	6	1	2
1	6	4	9	3	2	7	5	8
9	8	2	6	5	1	4	7	3
5	7	1	3	2	4	8	9	6
4	3	6	8	9	7	1	2	5
6	4	3	5	1	9	2	8	7
2	1	8	7	4	3	5	6	9
7	9	5	2	8	6	3	4	1

EASY

6	4	9	7	8	3	1	2	5
7	8	2	4	5	1	9	3	6
5	1	3	9	2	6	4	8	7
9	2	5	8	6	4	7	1	3
8	3	7	5	1	9	6	4	2
1	6	4	2	3	7	5	9	8
2	7	1	3	4	5	8	6	9
4	9	8	6	7	2	3	5	1
3	5	6	1	9	8	2	7	4

MEDIUM

3	7	2	1	8	4	9	6	5
5	4	1	9	7	6	2	8	3
8	6	9	5	3	2	4	7	1
2	9	7	3	1	8	5	4	6
6	5	8	4	9	7	1	3	2
1	3	4	6	2	5	7	9	8
9	1	5	7	6	3	8	2	4
4	8	3	2	5	9	6	1	7
7	2	6	8	4	1	3	5	9

MEDIUM

1	3	6	7	4	5	2	8	9
7	8	5	9	2	3	4	6	1
4	2	9	6	8	1	5	3	7
3	7	8	5	6	4	9	1	2
5	9	4	8	1	2	6	7	3
2	6	1	3	9	7	8	4	5
8	1	2	4	3	9	7	5	6
6	5	3	2	7	8	1	9	4
9	4	7	1	5	6	3	2	8

HARD

3	2	1	4	6	7	5	8	9
6	7	9	2	8	5	3	1	4
5	8	4	9	3	1	2	7	6
8	3	6	7	5	2	4	9	1
2	9	7	8	1	4	6	5	3
1	4	5	6	9	3	8	2	7
7	5	2	3	4	9	1	6	8
4	1	8	5	7	6	9	3	2
9	6	3	1	2	8	7	4	5

HARD

79 LIVERPOOL TO CARDIFF ROAD CHAT

A5080, M62, M6, M5, M50, A40, M4, A470

80 DC SUPERHEROES WORD SCRAMBLE

1. Hawkgirl **2.** Aquaman
3. The Flash **4.** Wonder Woman
5. Superman **6.** Supergirl
7. Bumblebee **8.** Batman

81 PECULIAR PLACES MATCHING GAME

United States – Accident
United States – Barbecue
Turkey – Batman
England – Catbrain
Puerto Rico – Dead Dog Beach
French Polynesia – Disappointment Islands
Greece – Drama
Central Latvia – Ogre

82 WORLD CUP TRIVIA

1. Italy. **2.** Not have a World Cup Final.
3. Uruguay, Italy, England and West Germany.
4. 1966. **5.** Every 4 years.
6. Spain. **7.** 7. **8.** Oleg Salenko. **9.** Vittorio Pozzo (Italy). **10.** Italy and Brazil.

84 WORLD LEADERS WORD SEARCH

86 TYPES OF RED WINE CROSSWORD

88 SUDOKU SUPERSTAR

2	8	4	9	6	1	5	7	3
7	6	5	3	2	8	1	9	4
3	1	9	4	7	5	8	2	6
6	5	2	1	3	4	7	8	9
8	3	7	5	9	2	4	6	1
9	4	1	6	8	7	3	5	2
4	7	6	2	5	3	9	1	8
5	2	3	8	1	9	6	4	7
1	9	8	7	4	6	2	3	5

EASY

2	8	6	9	7	3	5	1	4
1	9	3	4	5	6	2	7	8
5	4	7	8	2	1	3	6	9
9	7	2	3	1	4	6	8	5
4	5	1	6	8	7	9	3	2
6	3	8	5	9	2	1	4	7
3	6	9	7	4	5	8	2	1
7	1	5	2	3	8	4	9	6
8	2	4	1	6	9	7	5	3

EASY

6	2	7	4	1	9	5	8	3
8	1	4	3	6	5	2	7	9
5	9	3	2	7	8	1	4	6
3	6	8	9	4	1	7	5	2
2	5	1	8	3	7	6	9	4
7	4	9	6	5	2	3	1	8
1	8	6	5	9	3	4	2	7
9	3	5	7	2	4	8	6	1
4	7	2	1	8	6	9	3	5

MEDIUM

6	9	3	4	1	2	8	7	5
4	1	8	7	3	5	6	9	2
2	7	5	8	6	9	1	3	4
9	5	6	3	4	8	7	2	1
7	4	2	6	9	1	3	5	8
3	8	1	5	2	7	4	6	9
5	3	9	1	7	4	2	8	6
1	2	7	9	8	6	5	4	3
8	6	4	2	5	3	9	1	7

MEDIUM

5	8	1	2	9	7	6	3	4
3	4	7	6	5	8	1	2	9
9	6	2	1	3	4	8	7	5
2	5	4	8	1	9	7	6	3
7	3	6	5	4	2	9	1	8
8	1	9	3	7	6	5	4	2
6	7	8	4	2	5	3	9	1
4	9	3	7	8	1	2	5	6
1	2	5	9	6	3	4	8	7

HARD

1	3	6	2	5	9	4	7	8
2	8	7	3	4	6	9	5	1
5	9	4	7	8	1	2	6	3
3	5	2	9	1	7	6	8	4
7	4	1	8	6	3	5	9	2
8	6	9	4	2	5	1	3	7
4	7	3	6	9	2	8	1	5
9	2	5	1	3	8	7	4	6
6	1	8	5	7	4	3	2	9

HARD

89 CRIME AUTHORS WORD SCRAMBLE

1. Agatha Christie **2.** Ruth Rendell **3.** James Patterson **4.** Stieg Larsson **5.** John le Carré **6.** Stephen King **7.** Ian Rankin **8.** Lee Child

90 SPOT THE DIFFERENCE

92 SEVEN WONDERS OF THE WORLD SMART SEQUENCE

1. Colossus of Rhodes
2. Great Pyramid of Giza
3. Hanging Gardens of Babylon
4. Lighthouse of Alexandria
5. Mausoleum at Halicarnassus
6. Statue of Zeus at Olympia
7. Temple of Artemis at Ephesus

93 ROMAN GODS WORD SEARCH

M	H	Y	N	E	M	E	S	I	S	K	D	S	M	R
G	D	B	G	S	Y	J	I	U	L	G	H	D	Z	Q
L	D	W	Q	K	I	U	O	H	E	E	D	D	U	
A	V	R	E	N	I	M	H	B	P	O	R	L	K	E
G	Z	N	U	G	I	N	R	Z	U	W	C	I	R	I
M	S	G	R	F	G	L	A	P	H	B	U	A	G	L
Q	A	G	E	S	G	P	I	C	M	C	L	B	O	
L	T	R	N	B	D	D	T	V	L	I	E	R	D	Z
L	T	O	S	Y	F	X	D	I	T	U	S	E	Z	
C	F	V	L	A	O	W	O	Z	R	X	Y	S	R	Y
V	T	X	U	L	C	T	I	E	L	M	E	F	D	Y
Q	F	N	A	N	Q	L	Q	I	T	R	G	K	Q	A
B	A	S	Q	G	D	R	J	T	E	I	S	C	A	Z
N	E	P	T	U	N	E	A	X	O	G	A	A	D	
C	L	N	S	C	V	C	O	B	B	O	C	I	E	C

96 SPOT THE DIFFERENCE

94 RANDOM RECORD BREAKERS TRUE OR FALSE

1. False. The largest was made from 700,000.
2. True. 3. True. His name is Sultan Kösen. 4. True.
5. False. 'The sixth sick sheik's sixth sheep's sick' is listed as the world's hardest tongue twister in the Guinness Book of World Records. 6. True.
7. False. He is famous for running the longest distance of 38 feet and 8 inches while carrying a 26lb table with a 110lb woman sat on top of it in his mouth. 8. True.
9. True. 1,010 bikini-clad women took part.
10. True.

98 BEST BRITISH ALES CROSSWORD

```
              H
      I       O
      P    N  P
      H A R V E Y S
              W
  S T I C K Y W I C K E T           H
              A                     O
      B I S H O P S F I N G E R     B
              T                     G
      S P I T F I R E               O
              L                     B
      D O O M B A R                 L
              R O L D C R A F T Y H E N
              O
      L O N D O N P R I D E
  O L D S P E C K L E D H E N
              E
```

100 ROCK MUSIC TRIVIA

1. Definitely Maybe
2. 23 million **3.** Sting
4. Don't Be Cruel
5. Richard Stareky **6.** John
Entwhistle **7.** 4 **8.** Jimi
Hendrix **9.** Zakk Wylde
10. Knighthood
11. Elizabeth Taylor

102 WHITE WINE WORD SCRAMBLE

1. Chardonnay **2.** Pinot
Grigio **3.** Vermentino
4. Picpoul de Pinet
5. Chenin Blanc
6. White Rioja **7.** Muscat
8. Riesling

104 60s POP BANDS CROSSWORD

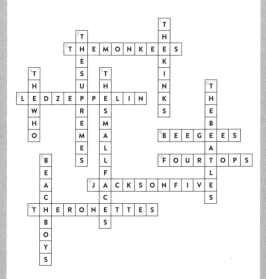

103 CAPITAL CITIES WORD SEARCH

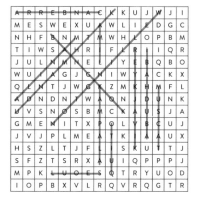

106 SPOT THE DIFFERENCE

110 SUDOKU SUPERSTAR

EASY

1	3	4	5	2	6	7	9	8
7	2	5	4	8	9	6	1	3
6	9	8	3	7	1	4	2	5
4	7	3	2	5	8	1	6	9
5	1	9	6	3	4	8	7	2
8	6	2	9	1	7	5	3	4
3	8	7	1	9	5	2	4	6
9	4	1	8	6	2	3	5	7
2	5	6	7	4	3	9	8	1

EASY

4	2	3	9	1	6	5	8	7
5	6	1	3	8	7	2	9	4
7	8	9	5	4	2	6	1	3
6	1	4	7	2	9	8	3	5
8	3	7	4	5	1	9	2	6
9	5	2	8	6	3	7	4	1
2	9	6	1	3	5	4	7	8
1	4	5	2	7	8	3	6	9
3	7	8	6	9	4	1	5	2

MEDIUM

9	2	8	4	3	1	7	5	6
5	4	1	7	6	2	3	8	9
7	3	6	9	5	8	1	2	4
3	7	4	2	9	5	8	6	1
1	6	2	8	4	7	9	3	5
8	5	9	6	1	3	4	7	2
6	8	7	1	2	9	5	4	3
2	1	3	5	7	4	6	9	8
4	9	5	3	8	6	2	1	7

MEDIUM

5	6	7	1	9	4	2	3	8
1	3	8	5	2	6	7	9	4
9	2	4	7	8	3	6	1	5
6	1	3	8	5	7	9	4	2
7	8	9	3	4	2	1	5	6
2	4	5	9	6	1	3	8	7
8	5	1	6	7	9	4	2	3
3	7	2	4	1	5	8	6	9
4	9	6	2	3	8	5	7	1

HARD

7	4	1	2	3	6	5	9	8
5	8	6	9	4	1	3	2	7
3	9	2	5	7	8	6	4	1
4	2	5	3	1	7	9	8	6
8	3	7	6	9	2	1	5	4
1	6	9	8	5	4	2	7	3
6	5	4	1	8	9	7	3	2
2	7	3	4	6	5	8	1	9
9	1	8	7	2	3	4	6	5

HARD

5	4	3	7	9	8	2	6	1
1	8	2	4	5	6	3	7	9
9	6	7	1	3	2	5	4	8
6	5	9	2	7	3	1	8	4
8	2	1	5	4	9	7	3	6
3	7	4	8	6	1	9	2	5
7	9	5	3	8	4	6	1	2
2	3	8	6	1	5	4	9	7
4	1	6	9	2	7	8	5	3

---

108 ROCK 'N' ROLL TRUE OR FALSE

1. True. Both were born on the 5th of November.
2. True. **3.** True. **4.** True.
5. False. Chip Taylor did write "Wild Thing." but he is Angelina Jolie's uncle.
6. False. Robert Allen Zimmerman briefly went by Elston Gunn before he renamed himself Bob Dylan.
7. True. **8.** True. **9.** False.
10. False. They were the first act to achieve the feat in UK chart history and the only act to do it twice.

---

111 MYTHICAL BEASTS WORD SEARCH

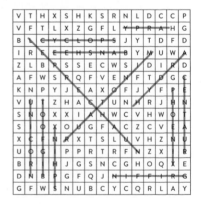